CELEBRATING THE CITY OF XIAMEN

Celebrating the City of Xiamen

Walter the Educator

Silent King Books
A WhichHead Entertainment Imprint

Copyright © 2024 by Walter the Educator

All rights reserved. No part of this book may be reproduced in any manner whatsoever without written per- mission except in the case of brief quotations embodied in critical articles and reviews.

First Printing, 2024

Disclaimer

This book is a literary work; the story is not about specific persons, locations, situations, and/or circumstances unless mentioned in a historical context. Any resemblance to real persons, locations, situations, and/or circumstances is coincidental. This book is for entertainment and informational purposes only. The author and publisher offer this information without warranties expressed or implied. No matter the grounds, neither the author nor the publisher will be accountable for any losses, injuries, or other damages caused by the reader's use of this book. The use of this book acknowledges an understanding and acceptance of this disclaimer.

Celebrating the City of Xiamen is a little collectible souvenir book that belongs to the Celebrating Cities Book Series by Walter the Educator. Collect them all and more books at WaltertheEducator.com

USE THE EXTRA SPACE TO TAKE NOTES AND DOCUMENT YOUR MEMORIES

XIAMEN

In the heart where tides embrace the shore,

Celebrating the City of Xiamen

Where Gulangyu's whispers weave folklore,

Xiamen rises, a jewel of the sea,

A city where the waves sing history.

Hulishan's cannons, silent now,

Guardians of peace with a solemn vow,

The fort that once saw battles' flame,

Now stands as a reminder of peace's name.

On the waters of Yundang Bay,

Reflections dance in the break of day,

Skylines rise, kissed by dawn's embrace,

Celebrating the City of

Xiamen

Mirroring dreams in their serene grace.

Markets buzz with vibrant life,

The pulse of commerce, free from strife,

Colors blend in a fragrant swirl,

Where cultures meet and traditions twirl.

Fujian tulou, round and grand,

Echoes of home, a crafted hand,

Communities built in a perfect ring,

Stories of unity their walls sing.

The beaches stretch, golden and pure,

Where waves and laughter intertwine, sure,

The sun bestows its gentle rays,

Blessing the shores in warm displays.

At night, the city's lights ignite,

A symphony of stars in urban flight,

Celebrating the City of Xiamen

Xiamen breathes with a rhythmic beat,

A harmony of the ancient and the sweet.

In every park where flowers bloom,

In every street where life finds room,

Xiamen's spirit, vibrant and free,

Flows like the tides, eternally.

A fusion of past and present's glow,

Where history's roots and futures grow,

A city, a song, a tale retold,

In Xiamen's heart, pure gold.

Celebrating the City of Xiamen

Celebrate this city by the sea,

Where every corner holds a memory,

In Xiamen's embrace, where dreams reside,

A place of wonder, and endless pride.

ABOUT THE CREATOR

Walter the Educator is one of the pseudonyms for Walter Anderson. Formally educated in Chemistry, Business, and Education, he is an educator, an author, a diverse entrepreneur, and he is the son of a disabled war veteran. "Walter the Educator" shares his time between educating and creating. He holds interests and owns several creative projects that entertain, enlighten, enhance, and educate, hoping to inspire and motivate you. Follow, find new works, and stay up to date with Walter the Educator™ at WaltertheEducator.com

www.ingramcontent.com/pod-product-compliance
Lightning Source LLC
LaVergne TN
LVHW012051070526
838201LV00082B/3905